joy

Other Studies in the Fruit of the Spirit Bible Study Series

Faithfulness: The Foundation of True Friendship
Gentleness: The Strength of Being Tender
Kindness: Reaching Out to Others
Love: Building Healthy Relationships
Patience: The Benefits of Waiting
Peace: Overcoming Anxiety and Conflict
Self-Control: Mastering Our Passions

joy

How to Rejoice in Any Situation

Phyllis J. Le Peau

GRAND RAPIDS, MICHIGAN 49530

ZONDERVAN™

Joy: How to Rejoice in Any Situation

Requests for information should be addressed to:
Zondervan, *Grand Rapids, Michigan 49530*

ISBN 0-310-23865-X

Study 1 is adapted from a study in *James: Faith That Works* in the LifeGuide Bible Study series from InterVarsity Press and is used by permission.

Interior design by Melissa Elenbaas

Printed in the United States of America

03 04 05 06 /❖ CH/ 10 9 8 7 6 5

CONTENTS

FRUIT OF THE SPIRIT BIBLE STUDIES

Welcome to Fruit of the Spirit Bible Studies. This series was written with one goal in mind—to allow the Spirit of God to use the Word of God to produce his fruit in your life.

To get the most from this series you need to understand a few basic facts:

Fruit of the Spirit Bible Studies are designed to be flexible. You can use them in your quiet times or for group discussion. They are ideal for Sunday school classes, small groups, or neighborhood Bible studies.

The eight guides in this series can be used in any order that is best for you or your group.

Because each guide contains only six studies, you can easily explore more than one fruit of the Spirit. In a Sunday school class, any two guides can be combined for a quarter (twelve weeks), or the entire series can be covered in a year.

Each study deliberately focuses on only one or two passages. That allows you to see each passage in its context, avoiding the temptation of prooftexting and the frustration of "Bible hopscotch" (jumping from verse to verse). If you would like to look up additional passages, a Bible concordance will give the most help.

The questions help you *discover* what the Bible says rather than simply *telling* you what it says. They encourage you to think and to explore options rather than to merely fill in the blanks with one-word answers.

Leader's notes are provided in the back of the guide. They show how to lead a group discussion, provide additional information on questions, and suggest ways to deal with problems that may come up in the discussion. With such helps, someone with little or no experience can lead an effective study.

SUGGESTIONS FOR INDIVIDUAL STUDY

1. Begin each study with prayer. Ask God to help you understand the passage and to apply it to your life.
2. A good modern translation, such as the *New International Version,* the *New American Standard Bible,* or the *Revised Standard Version,* will give you the most help. However, the questions in this guide are based on the *New International Version.*
3. Read and reread the passage(s). You must know what the passage says before you can understand what it means and how it applies to you.
4. Write your answers in the space provided in the study guide. This will help you to clearly express your understanding of the passage.
5. Keep a Bible dictionary handy. Use it to look up any unfamiliar words, names, or places.

SUGGESTIONS FOR GROUP STUDY

1. Come to the study prepared. Careful preparation will greatly enrich your time in group discussion.
2. Be willing to join in the discussion. The leader of the group will not be lecturing but will encourage people to discuss what they have learned in the passage. Plan to share what God has taught you in your individual study.
3. Stick to the passage being studied. Base your answers on the verses being discussed rather than on outside authorities such as commentaries or your favorite author or speaker.
4. Try to be sensitive to the other members of the group. Listen attentively when they speak, and be affirming whenever you can. This will encourage more hesitant members of the group to participate.
5. Be careful not to dominate the discussion. By all means, participate! But allow others to have equal time.
6. If you are the discussion leader, you will find additional suggestions and helpful ideas in the leader's notes at the back of the guide.

JOY

How to Rejoice in Any Situation

While hunting buffalo in the Dakota Badlands, Theodore Roosevelt spent two weeks in intense heat and driving rain. He got a deep gash in his forehead when his horse reared up unexpectedly. As he crawled on his belly to get a shot at an animal, he accidentally placed his hand on a cactus and received a fistful of spines. That evening he and his guide were rudely awakened by a cold rain that left them lying in four inches of water. Shivering between sodden blankets, the guide heard Roosevelt exclaim, "By Godfrey, but this is fun!"

Joy is found in the strangest of places—in hospital rooms where patients are weak from surgery, around a dinner table when a husband announces he has been laid off, or in a household where a parent's only companions are little children and the mundane tasks include laundry, cleaning, shopping, and cooking. Although situations like these are seldom "fun," they can be surprising occasions of joy.

How is this possible? The answer is found in two of my favorite songs, "The Joy of the Lord Is My Strength" and "In Thy Presence There Is Fullness of Joy." In my mind they summarize the truth about joy. It is possible to experience joy in the midst of trial, in the midst of weakness, even in the midst of deep pain—because none of these takes us out of God's presence. In fact, they can cause us to go deeper and deeper into his presence. There we find joy. And there we are strengthened by joy.

This may sound simplistic. But I have seen it happen. I have been strengthened by being around those who overflow with joy, whose outlook on the mundane things of life has been transformed by the joy of the Lord. Instead of boredom and complaint, there is life and vibrance.

And I have seen those in the midst of deep pain, whose world has caved in on them—such as a young man whose wife and unborn child were killed in a car crash—survive on the joy of the Lord. In excruciating agony, he knows "it is well" because the Lord is near. When all of his own physical, emotional, and spiritual strength are drained from his being, the Holy Spirit continues faithfully to produce the fruit of joy.

This Fruit of the Spirit Bible study looks at situations in which joy does not come naturally. The only explanation is that it is a work of the Spirit—joy in trials, joy in weakness, and joy in the gospel (when it involves great personal cost). We will also look at sources of joy—or ways of entering God's presence—joy in the Word, joy in God's discipline, and joy in Christ's rest.

God wants to make us like his Son, "who for the joy set before him, endured the cross." As you consider what the Scriptures say about the fruit of joy, my prayer is that it will fill your life in unexpected places.

JOY IN TRIALS

James 1:2–12

Saved alone" was the message that Horatio Spafford received from his wife after the ship sank that was taking her and their four children to England in November 1873. After reuniting with his grieving wife at sea, the boat came near the area where his children had drowned. It is speculated that at that time he wrote the words that vividly described his own grief and faith:

> When sorrows like sea billows roll–
> Whatever my lot
> Thou hast taught me to say,
> It is well, it is well with my soul.

Sorrow is a natural response to trials. But in James 1:2–12 we discover why even in the darkest times of our lives we can say with convincing clarity, "It is well with my soul!"

Warming Up

1. How does joy differ from happiness?

Digging In

2. Read James 1:2–12. It seems strange that we should "consider it pure joy . . . whenever [we] face trials of many kinds." Why are we to be joyful?

3. What is perseverance?

Why is it important in the Christian life?

4. How are perseverance and maturity developed in us by enduring trials (vv. 3–4)?

How does our attitude toward these trials affect our growth?

5. How do trials reveal the depth of our character?

What difficult experiences have increased your perseverance and maturity?

6. How might trials expose our need for God's wisdom (v. 5)?

7. According to James, how will God respond to our request for wisdom (v. 5)?

How is this promise a source of joy for you?

8. Under pressure, how does the faithful Christian (vv. 5–6) contrast with the person described in verses 6–8?

9. In the context of trials and perseverance, why does James contrast rich and poor Christians (vv. 9–11)?

10. In what ways do you rely on your possessions for joy?

11. In verse 12 we discover that there is a crown of life for those who persevere in trials. What is a crown of life?

    How can the promise of receiving this crown increase our joy in the midst of trials?

Pray about It

Praise God that this passage gives Christians an eternal perspective on trials and suffering. Ask him to make this perspective your perspective as you talk to him about trials and suffering in your life. Pray that you would truly experience joy in trials.

TAKING THE NEXT STEP

Each day look closely at one of the following passages of Scripture. They each contain truth about joy in trials. Read the passage, writing down the truths from it and how they relate to your own life and situation. Ask God to integrate the truth of these passages into your heart and mind so that you will live a life of joy in trials.

Matthew 21:18–22
John 15:18–25
John 16:33
John 1:1–13
Romans 5:1–5
1 Peter 1:3–9
1 Peter 4:12–16

JOY IN WEAKNESS

2 Corinthians 12:1–10

It had been a long time since I had felt this weak and helpless. In tears I shared my distress with my husband, Andy. I was struggling in a couple of relationships. Everything I did seemed to hurt the people I was trying to love. Besides that, I felt I was not growing spiritually. Though my goal for the year was to grow as a person of prayer, my prayer life was at an all-time low. I felt like a miserable failure.

When I was finished, Andy said gently, "You could be in no better place before God. He is much freer to work in us when we are at the end of ourselves."

In 2 Corinthians 12, Paul struggles with a painful weakness but discovers how it can become a source of strength and joy.

Warming Up

1. When you think of God's power, what comes to mind?

Digging In

2. Read 2 Corinthians 12:1–10. Paul feels forced to "boast" to defend himself against his opponents. How would you summarize his boasting (vv. 1–6)?

3. Why do you think he refers to "a man in Christ" (v. 2) when speaking about his own experience of being "caught up to paradise"?

4. In spite of his supernatural experiences, Paul wanted people to judge him on his character, not his experiences (v. 6). Why do people's actions and words reveal more about them than their "credentials"?

5. Why was Paul given a thorn in the flesh (v. 7)?

6. How can our experiences—spiritual and otherwise—lead us to become conceited?

7. Why did God refuse to remove Paul's thorn in spite of his repeated prayers (vv. 8–9)?

8. We usually want God to demonstrate his power by *removing* our weaknesses. Why is his power more perfectly revealed *in the midst of* our weaknesses?

9. When have you experienced God's power and sufficient grace in the midst of a painful weakness?

10. What different kinds of experiences qualify as "thorns" in our lives (v. 10)?

11. What thorn is currently causing you pain?

12. What have you learned from this passage that will help you to rejoice in that weakness?

Pray about It

Praise God that weakness has purpose in your life because you belong to the Lord Jesus Christ. Thank him for the ways that you have seen his strength through your weakness.

TAKING THE NEXT STEP

Simon Peter is one of many characters in Scripture who experienced weakness and failure that was turned into strength because of God's power. Look at his life closely through the following passages: Luke 5:1–11; 22:31; John 13:1–9, 31–38; Luke 22:54–62; John 21:15–19. Then respond to these questions.

What do you see of Jesus' vision for Peter?
What do you see of Peter's love for and loyalty to Jesus?
In what ways do you see Peter weak and inconsistent?
Why was it important that Peter's self-confidence and pride be broken?
How do you identify with Peter?
What is Jesus' response to Peter's weakness and failure?
What encouragement do you take as you reflect on 1 Peter 5:8–11?

JOY IN GOD'S WORD

Psalm 119:9–16, 105–112

In her book *The Joy of Discovery,* Oletta Wald writes, "While a student at the former Biblical Seminary in New York, I was taught how to explore the truths of the Bible in a methodical and systematic way. . . . I found that it was like working a combination lock. When I followed the steps, the Word opened up to me. I felt free. I realized that I was no longer dependent on others to gain insights into Scripture. I had become a discoverer. In a new way, Bible study had become more meaningful and personal. Most of all it was deeply satisfying to know how to discover the truths in God's Word. I had experienced the joy of discovery in Bible study!"

Centuries earlier the psalmist wrote of his own feelings about Scripture. It brought him such joy that he wrote 176 verses describing his response to it. We will look at just a few of those verses in this study as we consider what it means to have joy in God's Word.

Warming Up

1. If you were to describe your times in Scripture as eating food, what kind of food would it be—blueberry pie, meat and potatoes, green vegetables, whole-grain bread, chicken broth, or what? Explain.

Digging In

2. Read Psalm 119:9–16. How is the psalmist's passion for God's Word evident in these verses?

3. Describe a time when you rejoiced in the Word as one rejoices in great riches.

4. What are the functions of the Word of God according to this passage?

5. One of the functions of God's Word is to keep our way pure. What does a pure life depend on according to this passage (vv. 10–16)?

6. In what ways have you found it easy to live a pure life according to God's Word?

How have you found it difficult?

7. Read Psalm 119:105–112. Another major function of the Scriptures is guidance (v. 105). In what areas do you rely on God's Word for guidance?

8. What difficulties has the psalmist encountered in following God's Word?

9. In spite of his suffering, how does the psalmist feel about Scripture?

10. How do your responses to Scripture compare to those of the psalmist in both of these passages (vv. 9–16, 105–112)?

11. The psalmist makes a purposeful choice not to neglect God's Word (v. 16). What choices do you need to make in order for God's Word to play a more vital role in your life?

Pray about It

The psalmist says that the Scriptures are "the joy of my heart." Pray that God will bring joy to your heart as you keep the commitments you have made regarding his Word.

TAKING THE NEXT STEP

Continue your meditation on the Word of God this week by reflecting on Psalm 119:1–8, 17–24.

After reading verses 1–8, divide a sheet of paper into three columns. In the first column list all the effects of the Word of God in one's life as stated by the passage. In the next column write how you have experienced each, and in the final column, how you would like to grow in experiencing each.

Read verses 17–24. List from this passage all that the psalmist asks of God concerning his Word. Ask God to do these things in you. Then, throughout the coming weeks, write down his answers to your requests.

JOY IN THE GOSPEL

Philippians 1:3–26

Debby was captured by guerrilla forces. She was a young missionary nurse, pregnant with her third child. Though her captors were a threat to her life and that of her unborn child, she prayed for them. Even as she feared death, she experienced joy because she saw the gospel at work in the very people who had imprisoned her. In the midst of those awful circumstances, her first concern was that Christ be praised. Debby is a vital testimony of what it means to rejoice in the gospel of Jesus Christ.

We see this same joy in Paul as he desires for the gospel to advance, even at great personal cost.

Warming Up

1. Have you ever felt joy in the midst of difficult circumstances? If so, why?

Digging In

2. Read Philippians 1:3–26. According to these verses, what reasons might Paul have to feel discouraged or depressed (vv. 7, 12–14, 22)?

3. In spite of his personal circumstances, what reasons does Paul give for being joyful?

4. Joy usually results when our desires are fulfilled and our values are affirmed. What do we learn about Paul's values and desires in this passage?

5. Imagine that you are in Paul's situation—under armed guard, in chains, unable to leave your rented quarters, awaiting trial. How would you feel?

6. What difference would news of the spread of the gospel make in your feelings? (Be honest.) Explain.

7. How do your desires and values compare to Paul's?

8. Let's look more closely at the gospel in which Paul rejoices. What confidence does he have about the gospel (vv. 6–7)?

How do you respond to the assurance that God will complete the good work he has begun in you?

9. As God completes his good work in the Philippians and in us, what kind of people does Paul pray we will become (vv. 9–11)?

10. How much does your joy center on the work of the gospel in you and in others?

11. What substitutes for the gospel do we and our culture gravitate to for sources of joy?

How effective are they in producing joy? Explain.

12. Paul's joy in the gospel was so all-consuming that he proclaimed, "For me, to live is Christ and to die is gain" (v. 21). What do you need to experience that kind of joyful commitment to Christ?

Pray about It

Thank God for the gospel of Jesus Christ. Confess to him those areas in which your values and desires are not like Paul's. Thank him that he has promised to complete in you the work he began when you became a Christian.

TAKING THE NEXT STEP

During this next week make Paul's prayer for the Philippians your own.

First, make a list of the relationships where you need to love or love more deeply. Ask God to give insight you need about yourself and others in order for your love to grow. Ask him for strength to wrestle with the hard issues of these relationships. Pray that the light of Jesus and the knowledge of his gospel will change how you love others.

Then make a list of situations where you need to be pure and blameless. Ask the Lord to help you differentiate not only between good and evil, but between good and better, and better and best.

Finally, ask God to give you a life of fruitfulness as you participate in the gospel. Ask him to fill you with his joy.

JOY IN GOD'S DISCIPLINE

Hebrews 12:1–13

George Macdonald's short story "The Gifts of the Child Christ" describes a little girl who was very sad when she heard Hebrews 12:6, "Whom the Lord loveth, he chasteneth." She was from a well-to-do family and had suffered very little in life. Since she assumed she had not been disciplined by God, she concluded that he must not love her.

It is, of course, not necessary to draw such a conclusion if God doesn't discipline us at certain times. Yet when God does discipline us, the author of Hebrews gives us several reasons to rejoice.

Warming Up

1. How do children usually feel about being disciplined by their parents?

Digging In

2. Read Hebrews 12:1–13. The writer of Hebrews compares the Christian life to a race (vv. 1–3). What principles for running does he recommend (vv. 1–3)?

3. What kinds of "clothing" can hinder us, and what kinds of sins can entangle us as we run?

4. What does it mean to "fix our eyes on Jesus" (v. 2)?

5. How can focusing on Jesus affect your perseverance in running this race (vv. 2–4)?

6. What is encouraging about the fact that the Lord disciplines us (vv. 5–11)?

7. What do you think it means to "share in his holiness" (v. 10)?

8. The results of discipline are "a harvest of righteousness and peace" (v. 11). What might this look like in a person's life in concrete, practical ways?

9. In what sense is God's discipline like physical therapy (vv. 12–13)?

Why is it vital for us to cooperate in this therapy?

10. In what ways have you experienced God's discipline in your life?

11. How do you usually respond to God's discipline?

Pray about It

Praise God for what you have learned about our heavenly Father's discipline in this passage. Pray that he will help you to accept his discipline joyfully. Ask him to produce in you holiness and the fruit of righteousness and peace.

TAKING THE NEXT STEP

Rent the movie *Chariots of Fire.* As you view the movie jot down what you see of this passage in it. Consider such things as running the race, the effect of people in the stands cheering the runners on, laying aside weights that hinder and entangle, perseverance and discipline, and losing heart.

JOY IN CHRIST'S REST

Matthew 11:28–30

In his hymn "I Heard the Voice of Jesus Say," Horatius Bonar describes Jesus' invitation to the weary and burdened:

> I heard the voice of Jesus say, "Come unto me and rest:
> Lay down, thou weary one, lay down thy head upon my breast."
> I came to Jesus as I was, weary, and worn, and sad.
> I found in Him a resting-place, and He has made me glad.

There is a part of us that yearns for the rest that Jesus gives. Our lives are full of activity—activity that all too often seems empty and worthless. Quiet and solitude are unheard of. In the midst of our frenzied pace, Jesus continues to gently give the invitation: "Come to me and rest."

Warming Up

1. What are some of the deep longings of your heart? For what do you yearn?

Digging In

2. Read Matthew 11:28–30. What invitation does Jesus give in this passage?

3. What do you think it means to "come to Jesus"?

4. How easy or difficult is it for you to come to him? Why?

5. Jesus invites all who are weary and burdened (v. 28). What types of weariness and burdens might he have in mind?

6. To what extent do you identify with the weary and burdened? Explain.

7. What is a yoke (v. 29), and what does it do?

What does it mean, therefore, to take Christ's yoke upon us?

8. What promises does Jesus make to those who respond to his invitation?

9. What would it mean to you to find "rest for your soul"?

How would finding rest for your soul bring you joy?

10. How does it help you to know that Christ's yoke is easy and his burden is light (v. 30)?

11. Jesus describes himself as "gentle and humble in heart" (v. 29). How do these qualities increase your desire to come to him and learn from him?

12. How does the rest Jesus promises in this passage speak to the yearnings and longings of your heart?

Pray about It

Ask God to reveal to you specific ways you can respond to Jesus' invitation to rest. Thank him for the joy we have when we experience Christ's rest.

TAKING THE NEXT STEP

As you respond to Jesus' invitation to come to him throughout the weeks, reflect on Philippians 2:5–11. Ask Jesus to give you the rest that comes from making his mind and attitude your own. Ask him to deliver you from competition, pretense, and arrogance. Talk to him about the desire you have to freely serve others with joy. Praise him for who he is and because God has given him a name that is above every name.

LEADER'S NOTES

Leading a Bible discussion—especially for the first time—can make you feel both nervous and excited. If you are nervous, realize that you are in good company. Many biblical leaders, such as Moses, Joshua, and the apostle Paul, felt nervous and inadequate to lead others (see, for example, 1 Cor. 2:3). Yet God's grace was sufficient for them, just as it will be for you.

Some excitement is also natural. Your leadership is a gift to the others in the group. Keep in mind, however, that other group members also share responsibility for the group. Your role is simply to stimulate discussion by asking questions and encouraging people to respond. The suggestions listed below can help you to be an effective leader.

PREPARING TO LEAD

1. Ask God to help you understand and apply the passage to your own life. Unless that happens, you will not be prepared to lead others.
2. Carefully work through each question in the study guide. Meditate and reflect on the passage as you formulate your answers.
3. Familiarize yourself with the leader's notes for the study. These will help you understand the purpose of the study and will provide valuable information about the questions in the study.
4. Pray for the various members of the group. Ask God to use these studies to bring about greater spiritual fruit in the life of each person.

5. Before the first meeting, make sure each person has a study guide. Encourage them to prepare beforehand for each study.

LEADING THE STUDY

1. Begin the study on time. If people realize that the study begins on schedule, they will work harder to arrive on time.
2. At the beginning of your first time together, explain that these studies are designed to be discussions not lectures. Encourage everyone to participate, but realize that some may be hesitant to speak during the first few sessions.
3. Read the introductory paragraph at the beginning of the discussion. This will orient the group to the passage being studied.
4. Read the passage aloud. You may choose to do this yourself, or you might ask for volunteers.
5. The questions in the guide are designed to be used just as they are written. If you wish, you may simply read each one aloud to the group. Or you may prefer to express them in your own words. However, unnecessary rewording of the questions is not recommended.
6. Don't be afraid of silence. People in the group may need time to think before responding.
7. Avoid answering your own questions. If necessary, rephrase a question until it is clearly understood. Even an eager group will quickly become passive and silent if they think the leader will do most of the talking.
8. Encourage more than one answer to each question. Ask, "What do the rest of you think?" or "Anyone else?" until several people have had a chance to respond.
9. Try to be affirming whenever possible. Let people know you appreciate their insights into the passage.
10. Never reject an answer. If it is clearly wrong, ask, "Which verse led you to that conclusion?" Or let the group handle the problem by asking them what they think about the question.
11. Avoid going off on tangents. If people wander off course, gently bring them back to the passage being considered.

12. Conclude your time together with conversational prayer. Ask God to help you apply those things that you learned in the study.
13. End on time. This will be easier if you control the pace of the discussion by not spending too much time on some questions or too little on others.

Many more suggestions and helps are found in the book *Leading Bible Discussions* (InterVarsity Press). Reading that would be well worth your time.

Study 1

JOY IN TRIALS

James 1:2–12

Purpose: To understand how and why we can rejoice in trials.

Question 1. Every study begins with an "approach question," which is discussed *before* reading the passage. An approach question is designed to do three things.

First, it helps to break the ice. Because an approach question doesn't require any knowledge of the passage or any special preparation, it can get people talking and can help them to warm up to each other.

Second, an approach question can motivate people to study the passage at hand. At the beginning of the study, people in the group aren't necessarily ready to jump into the world of the Bible. Their minds may be on other things (their kids, a problem at work, an upcoming meeting) that have nothing to do with the study. An approach question can capture their interest and draw them into the discussion by raising important issues related to the study. The question becomes a bridge between their personal lives and the answers found in Scripture.

Third, a good approach question can reveal where people's thoughts or feelings need to be transformed by Scripture. That is why it is important to ask the approach question *before* reading the passage. The passage might inhibit the spontaneous, honest answers people might have given because they feel compelled to give biblical answers. The approach question allows them to compare their personal thoughts and feelings with what they later discover in Scripture.

Question 2. "Trials are seldom met with joy. However, James not only instructs us to face trials with joy, but with pure joy. In the Greek text, the word translated as pure is the word *pas,* which is a primary word meaning all, every, and whole or thoroughly.

"James is telling us not to 'fake it.' We should have a joy which is neither contrived or forced as some impossible religious obligation. To the contrary, we should have pure, unadulterated, all-encompassing, thorough joy! It should be the 'real thing.'

"The second word we should explore should be the word for 'trial,' from the Greek *peirasmos.* The root of this word means 'to assay, to examine, or to put to the proof.' A good Biblical and theological definition might be 'an external adversity which provides a testing towards an end.'

"For example, this is the word used to describe the exciting adventure of a young bird 'testing' his wings. It is the word often translated as 'temptation,' as in the prayer Jesus taught his disciples (Matt. 6:13). The writer of Hebrews uses the word to describe the trials or temptations faced by the Children of Israel (Heb. 3:8).

"One of the greatest promises regarding such trials or temptations is found in 1 Corinthians where Paul writes, 'No temptation (trial) has overtaken you except such as is common to man; but God is faithful, who will not allow you to be tempted beyond what you are able, but with the temptation will also make the way of escape, that you may be able to bear it' (1 Cor. 10:13). It is with this kind of joy, hope, and optimism that we should face the trials of life.

"A third word which we should explore in verse 2 is the word translated as 'various'. It is a form of the Greek word *poikilos,* which means many or several kinds of trials. In my study of the Word of God and in my pastoral counseling, I have discovered at least three varieties of trials or temptations which are faced by sincere Christians. . . . These are: the cause and effect trial, the spiritual trial and the spiritually mysterious trial" (Paul A. Cedar, *James, 1, 2, Peter, Jude,* The Communicator's Commentary [Waco, Tex.: Word Books, 1984], 19–21).

According to George Stulac there is a primary focus of trials that James speaks of in this passage. "It is not that Christians are the only ones who have ever been persecuted. Nor is the letter intended to give comfort to Christians who suffer as consequence of their own sin. . . .When he writes about 'trials,' he means hardships and sufferings that Christians

encounter even as they are following the Lord. . . . James will explicitly include poverty as one of the *trials of many kinds.* But he most particularly has in mind the trials of being persecuted, the trials that come as a consequence of one's faith in Christ" (George M. Stulac, *James,* The IVP New Testament Commentary Series [Downers Grove, Ill.: InterVarsity, 1993], 33).

Question 3. Perseverance is the ability to endure patiently. It means not giving up in trusting or praying—even when the need never seems to come to an end. It means discipline. Perseverance is obeying Christ when it is difficult and does not feel good. It requires faithfulness that is sturdy and steadfast.

Help your group to think through the importance of perseverance in the Christian life. Have them talk about situations from their own experience in which perseverance was needed. One of the more obvious places is prayer. Sometimes it does not feel good to pray, and there are no immediate results. Yet God asks us to persevere in prayer. Another area may be love. Sometimes it is not easy to love, but as followers of Jesus we must persevere in love. Perseverance has to do with continuing to do what is right even when there are no immediate results.

Question 4. "That testing *develops,* or 'produces,' perseverance is emphatic. It may be compared to 1:20, where human anger does not 'bring about' the righteous life that God desires . . . but the testing of genuine faith will certainly produce perserverance.

"James' earnestness needs to be heard with the very direct questions this raises. Don't you desire this quality of faith in yourself? Isn't it the desire of your heart to learn to live by faith and be 'a servant of God and of the Lord Jesus Christ' in a patient, disciplined, steadfast, faithful way? Now you have the reason to rejoice in the midst of trials! These trials provide the opportunity for the testing that will develop this quality of faith. To stop trusting and start worrying, to cease ministering and start withdrawing, to interrupt godliness and start selfishness, just because of one's anxiety over the current trials, would be precisely the wrong course to take. The spiritual realities call for joy in the opportunity to learn perseverance.

"Why would perseverance be so valuable? It is because there is a fourth stage in the spiritual progression: 'that you may be mature and complete, not lacking anything.' Perseverance turns out to be not the end in itself, but rather the lifestyle by which the servant of Jesus Christ attains maturity" (Stulac, *James,* 37–38).

"The secret lies not in Stoic courage or in weak collapse (cf. Heb. 12:5f.) but in knowledge James is sure that his readers know. If they are to profit by their knowledge, they should remember that the trials which embody the testing of your faith bring to light its reality and its power. This they know already. Let them dwell on it, realizing that faith preserved and practiced in trials leads on to victory and deeper joy. The outcome is steadfastness, the quality of 'staying put'—under the slings and arrows of outrageous fortune. Cf. Romans 5:3.

"James is not limiting himself to a single, isolated trial. Active resistance must continue always. The full effect is personal, for it means that through their steadfastness they will be perfect and complete. *Perfect* suggests a ripeness and maturity in contrast to an earlier weakness; *complete* implies a wholeness and freedom from blemish with no Christian virtue absent; but the two words should be taken together" (*The New Bible Commentary: Revised* [Grand Rapids, Mich.: Eerdmans, 1970], 1224).

In thinking about how perseverance and maturity are developed by enduring trials it is important to look at the phrase *consider it pure joy.* Our attitude and response to trials affects whether or not perseverance is indeed developed and then able to finish its work of maturity in us. Our attitude also affects our willingness to go to God for wisdom, another sign of maturity. A friend once said to me, "Maturity does not mean that I have no problems. It does mean that I know where to get help with my problems."

"In the light of this spiritual goal we can now return to the beginning of 1:2 and have an idea of what James means by *consider it pure joy*" (Stulac, *James,* 39).

Question 5. Be sure to look at how trials reveal the depth of our character before moving on to the specific experiences discussed in the second part of the question. Help your group look at how trials reveal what is in our character. For example, what do trials bring out in us that might

not be revealed when life is running smoothly? Trials reveal where we put our faith rather than where we *say* we put it.

Question 6. We do not by nature admit that we are in need and therefore do not freely ask for help or wisdom—even or especially from God. However, when we are in the midst of trials and do not know what to do, wisdom becomes of utmost importance. When we are suffering the cry of our heart often is, "I don't know what to do!" This awareness and desperation can drive us to asking God for wisdom, because trials expose our need for God's wisdom.

"In the face of such trials what should 'the servant of God and of the Lord Jesus Christ' do? *He should ask God* for the wisdom that is lacking. This is not to dismiss the problems with a simplistic solution, but it is to face the problems with the root solution" (Stulac, *James,* 41).

Question 8. This may elicit questions about the place of doubt in the Christian life. While periods of questioning can be healthy and allow for growth, a life characterized by indecisiveness is displeasing to God. James draws two extremes to make his point.

Question 9. "The illustrations of the poor and the rich do no more than drive this lesson home: each is exhorted to see his lot in the light of spiritual reality. . . . The one, against whom life's tides seem to be running, and who is *lowly* as this world reckons things, seeks to live in a sustained awareness of the heights to which he has been lifted in Christ. The other, with his rich supply of this world's goods, looks rather to the depths from which Christ has rescued him, where, but for the grace of God, he would still languish, and to which, in his own heart, he knows he is still prone" (Alec Motyer, *James* [Downers Grove, Ill.: InterVarsity, 1985], 43–44).

Question 10. Depending on the makeup of your group, you might want to change question 10 to, "How has good fortune turned you toward God?"

Question 11. In the New Testament the word "*stephanos* denotes properly a chaplet or a circlet. It is used of Christ's crown of thorns. . . . What is clear is that this 'crown' was a mocking symbol of royalty, perhaps also of divinity. But though the *stephanos* might denote a crown of royalty

(Rev. vi.2, etc.), its more usual use was for the laurel wreath awarded to the victor at the Games or for a festive garland used on occasions of rejoicing. These uses underlie most of the New Testament references. Thus Paul reminds the Corinthians that athletes strive 'to obtain a corruptible crown' and he adds, 'but we are incorruptible' (1 Cor. ix.25). . . . Sometimes the Christian's crown is here and now, as when Paul thinks of his converts as his crown (Phil. iv. 1; 1 Thes. ii.19). More usually it is in the hereafter, as the 'crown of righteousness, which the Lord, the righteous judge, shall give me at that day' (2 Tim. iv.8). There are references also to a 'crown of life' (Jas. i.12; Rev. ii.10) and also to 'a crown of glory that fadeth not away' (1 Pet. v.4)" (*The New Bible Dictionary* [Grand Rapids, Mich.: Eerdmans, 1962], 281).

Study 2

JOY IN WEAKNESS

2 Corinthians 12:1–10

Purpose: To discover how God uses weakness in our lives and why it is important to rejoice in it.

Question 2. Lead the group to look at why Paul is boasting, what he thinks this boasting will accomplish, why he does not like it, and what he will boast about.

"Paul now goes on to boast about his *visions and revelations from the Lord.* He is conscious that there is *nothing to be gained* by doing so, but much to be lost if he does not. Evidently his opponents had criticized his claim to be an apostle saying that he had not experienced visions and revelations. Paul puts the record straight" (*The New Bible Commentary* [Downers Grove, Ill.: InterVarsity, 1994], 1203).

"If we have any sensitiveness, we should read this passage with a certain reverence, for in it Paul lays bare his heart and shows us at one and the same time his glory and his pain.

"All against his will he is still setting out his credentials, and he tells of an experience at which we can only wonder and which we cannot even try to probe. . . .

"One lovely thing we may note, for it will help a little. The word *Paradise* comes from a Persian word which means *a walled-garden.* When a Persian king wished to confer a very special honour on someone especially dear to him, he made him *a companion of the garden* and gave him the right to walk in the royal gardens with him in intimate companionship. In this experience, as never before and never again, Paul had been the companion of God" (William Barclay, *The Letters to the Corinthians* [Philadelphia: Westminster Press, 1975], 256–57).

Question 3. "The somewhat enigmatic reference to himself as a man in Christ is due partly to his reluctance to speak about the subject, and partly to give the impression that any Christian (for a Christian cannot better be described than as 'a man in Christ') might have been privileged to experience this vision, while he alone could have experienced the special vision which was the means of his conversion" (R. V. G. Tasker, *The Second Epistle of Paul to the Corinthians,* Tyndale New Testament Commentaries [Grand Rapids, Mich.: Eerdmans, 1978], 170).

Question 4. It is amazing to reflect on Paul's words "so no one will think more of me than is warranted by what I do or say." Our tendency and that of people in our culture is to prove ourselves, to wave our credentials for all to see, and to actually be fearful of judgements others will make of us based on what we do or say.

Actions and words reveal more about people than credentials because words and actions reveal what is deep within our hearts and minds.

Question 5. "Paul interpreted the nagging satanic messenger as 'given' him to keep his feet on the ground, to keep him earthly and normal. . . . Paul's Christian experiences could have carried him away, elevated him over others, but the thorn nailed him to earth, as he twice expresses it, 'to keep me from being too elated.' . . .

"The power of Christ is power *in weakness;* all other power—i.e., power in power—Paul must have found puny in comparison. In this life, only power in weakness is divine and sure to keep divinity where it belongs—with God and not the vessel (II Cor. 4:7)" (Frederick Dale Bruner, *A Theology of the Holy Spirit* [Grand Rapids, Mich.: Eerdmans, 1970], 313–14).

Question 6. One of the points of this question is, What can we learn from this passage to avoid taking credit for what God is doing?

Question 7. "God promised Paul that in the midst of the weakness and frustration which this 'thorn' produced, he would find God's power all the more present. Having heard such a word from God, Paul is able to boast about weaknesses, not because he enjoys them but because he knows that the power of Christ rests upon him in his weaknesses. He

then goes on to apply this work of God to other areas of his life in which he confronts weakness and suffering, for *when I am weak, then I am strong*" (*The New Bible Commentary,* 1204).

Question 8. When we are not weak and needy, it is easy to think and live as if the power were our own. When the Lord meets us in our weakness, it is obviously his power and everyone knows it.

Question 10. Paul mentions a variety of experiences that would qualify as thorns: weaknesses, insults, hardships, persecutions, and difficulties (v. 10). You might ask the group to give specific examples of some of these. (Sins of any kind would not qualify as thorns, since God is *more than willing* to remove these from our lives.) Hardship that results from sin can be dealt with only through confession and repentance. Thorns in the flesh are not just simple inconveniences.

Study 3

JOY IN GOD'S WORD

Psalm 119:9–16, 105–112

Purpose: To understand that we can experience joy from God's Word by giving it concentrated time and obedience.

Of this psalm, Derek Kidner writes, "This giant among the Psalms shows the full flowering of that 'delight . . . in the law of the Lord' which is described in Psalm 1, and gives its personal witness to the many-sided qualities of Scripture praised in Psalm 19:7ff.

"This untiring emphasis has led some to accuse the psalmist of worshipping the Word rather than the Lord; but it has been well remarked that every reference here to Scripture, without exception, relates it explicitly to its author; indeed every verse from 4 to the end is a prayer or affirmation addressed to Him. This is true piety: a love of God not desiccated by study but refreshed, informed and nourished by it" (Derek Kidner, *Psalms 73–150,* Tyndale Old Testament Comentaries [London: Inter-Varsity, 1975], 416, 19).

Question 2. "Expressions like *I rejoice* (v. 14), *I meditate* (v. 15), and *I delight* all reveal the psalmist's personal intensity concerning God's Word. The author of this psalm was passionate about being watchful (9), devoted (10), committing the word to memory (11), looking to God for understanding (12), sharing the truth with others (13), subjecting his emotions to the love of God's word (14, 16), giving it concentrated attention (15)" (*The New Bible Commentary: Revised,* 527).

Question 3. It is important in this question to set an atmosphere for honesty. Certainly we do not always rejoice in Scripture as we would with great riches. There may be some in your group who have never had this experience. That is all right. The goal is not to make members feel they

have to have a victory story. It will be greatly encouraging, however, to hear about times when others have rejoiced in the Word. As the leader, you should be ready to share such an experience, if you have one.

Question 4. The Word keeps a person's way pure (v. 9), keeps us from straying from obedience (v. 10), keeps us from sin (v. 11), gives substance for praise (vv. 12–13), gives a basis for rejoicing and delight (vv. 14, 16), and supplies truth worth meditating on (v. 15).

Question 5. "The case posed of a young man, i.e., a situation where the life of purity is under constant pressure. The possibility of a pure life depends on the direction of the will (10), the contents of mind and memory (11), the pre-occupations of the mouth (13), and of the emotions (14, 16), the subjects of thought (15, 16). The outward life arises from inward factors, all absorbed in the word but centralized on the Lord in praise and instruction (12). Now, a practical question, 'By what means?' The problem is outward but the answer is inward" (*The New Bible Commentary,* 567).

Question 7. "Verses 105 and 106 together show what kind of *light* and *path* are in mind, and verse 104 makes it doubly clear. This is not convenient guidance for one's career, but truth for moral choices: see, for instance, the kind of 'snare' and 'straying' that are implied in 110. The classic example of light from Scripture, well used in a place of many snares, is our Lord's temptation" (Kidner, *Psalms 73–150,* 427).

Encourage people not just to think of the big decisions in life but to consider how God uses Scripture to guide them in daily matters of morality and important choices of life.

Question 9. "The practical usefulness of the word as a guide (105) . . . makes the psalmist solemnly determined (106, 111, 112) to hold to it, in trouble (107), joy (108), peril (109), hostility (110). . . .

"The words *Feet . . . path* possibly suggest 'for the next step as well as for the more remote destination'" (*The New Bible Commentary: Revised,* 528).

Study 4

JOY IN THE GOSPEL

Philippians 1:3–26

Purpose: To see how the spread of the gospel of Christ is central to Paul's joy. To make Christ and the good news about him more central to our joy.

"The church at Philippi was Paul's '***joy*** and crown' (4:1). Of all his churches it gave him the least trouble, perhaps no trouble at all, and the most satisfaction. So Philippians is a letter of ***joy,*** brimming over with expressions of gratitude, affection, and love.

"Philippians is also a letter desperately needed by the modern church. It provides a picture of a church that takes seriously who she is as partners with Christ in the Gospel, who accepts Jesus as Lord and patterns her ministry after Him—'taking the form of servant,' always exalting the Lord and being strengthened by Him, living in hope 'that He who has begun a good work in you will complete it' (vs. 6), expressing the fruits of the Spirit, living as a witnesses to our servant-Lord on earth, but knowing our citizenship is in heaven" (Maxie D. Dunnam, *Galatians, Ephesians, Philippians, Colossians, Philemon,* The Communicator's Commentary [Waco, Tex.: Word Books, 1982], 251).

Before beginning this study on joy in the gospel, it might be good to challenge a popular misconception. Jack Kuhatschek writes, "People often say that happiness is dependent on circumstances and joy is not. I don't believe it. I think joy is just as dependent on circumstances as happiness, and I believe Paul would not have been opposed to saying he was 'happy' about what was happening in Philippi. Joy results from seeing our desires fulfilled. Paul was able to be joyful even in prison because his greatest desires centered on the gospel, not his personal comfort. The difference, therefore, between Paul and us is one of values and desires—we

often value our personal comfort most; he valued the gospel. What we need, then, is a shift in values. The claim that joy must somehow be independent of circumstances is a red herring" (unpublished letter to the author).

Question 3. "Every time Paul thinks of his friends in Philippi, he is filled with joy. The entire letter throbs with personal intensity. . . . Affection, gratitude, confidence, and *joy* fill the mind of Paul, even though he is in prison, as he thinks of the one church which never caused him trouble or anxiety.

"While a number of themes are woven into the first chapter, they may all fall under the theme *partnership in the gospel*" (Dunnam, *Galatians, Ephesians, Philippians, Colossians, Philemon,* 257).

Paul experiences joy for the following reasons: because of the Philippians' partnership in the gospel (v. 5), because God will complete the work in them that he began (v. 6), because of their fellowship in the gospel with him (v. 7), because the gospel has been advanced (v. 12), because the Word of God has been spoken out more courageously (v. 14), because Christ is preached (v. 18), and because Christ will be exalted in his body (vv. 20–26). To live is Christ, fruitful labor, their progress and joy in the faith and their joy in Christ Jesus will overflow and to die is gain.

"People are often amazed that Paul is able to be joyful in the midst of such difficult circumstances. Yet verses 20–21 help us to understand the reason for his joy. If he were living merely for his own happiness and pleasure, then his joy would be senseless" (Donald Baker, *Philippians: Jesus Our Joy,* A LifeGuide Bible Study [Downers Grove, Ill.: InterVarsity, 1985], 53).

Question 4. "Because he was living for Jesus Christ and the advancement of his kingdom, Paul had reason for joy: Jesus Christ was being preached and exalted because of Paul's imprisonment" (Baker, *Philippians: Jesus Our Joy,* 53).

Question 7. Paul's joy often seems baffling to us because we fail to realize how closely our joy is linked to our personal desires and values. If we want to experience Paul's joy, then we must make Jesus Christ and his gospel our greatest desire and our supreme value. Only then will we be able to find joy in the midst of the kind of circumstances Paul faced. As long as we value our personal comfort and pleasure most in life, our joy will always be enslaved to our personal circumstances.

Question 9. "*It is a prayer for love. 'That your love may abound still more'* (v 9). It is on target that this would be Paul's great intercession for those who are participants in the gospel, because love is the core word of the gospel. In English, 'love' is an appallingly overworked word, diminishished in power. The Greek words for immoral passion, sexual feeling, fraternal and family affection are all translated 'love.' A fourth Greek word for love was lifted out of obscurity into immortality by the New Testament. Writers like John and Paul selected that word for the love expressed in what God chose to do in Jesus Christ. The spontaneous, unmerited love and favor God has shown us rebellious and pride-filled creatures is *agape*: 'The Son of God loved me and gave Himself for me.'

"*It is a prayer for light. 'That your love may abound still more and more in knowledge and all discernment.'*

"Who coined the phrase that 'love is blind!' That is 180 degrees off course. In this verse we separate light from love only for the sake of clear reflection. Paul's prayer shows us that we can hardly pray for growing love apart from a greatening light. Both the Phillips rendering and the NEB make this sublimely clear. 'My prayer for you is that you may have still more love—a love that is full of knowledge and every wise insight' (Phillips). 'And this is my prayer , that your love may grow ever richer and richer in knowledge and insight of every kind' (NEB).

"Love calls for and seeks after knowledge. It is not blind. It does not overlook faults and weaknesses in others, but sees them clearly, looking beyond them to 'the heart of things' and continuing to love. Love does not downplay truth, or speak in circles or opaquely to avoid confrontation, but speaks the truth that change and healing may be possible.

"*It is a prayer for life.* Everything that Christ does in us must reflect itself through us. So the prayer is for life, life lived in a special way because the love of Christ is abounding within us, spiritual knowledge is increasing, and the capacity of discernment is being sharpened. How does this life express itself practically? What does it look like? '*That you may approve things that are excellent*' (v 10). Is the word *discriminating?* To be able to

differentiate not only between good and evil, but between good and better, between better and the best. *Excellence* is the quality we must seek.

"*'Being filled with the fruits of righteousness.'* This is a beautiful expression for our life as participants in the gospel: *fruitfulness.* We would expect Paul to pray in this fashion. He knew the work of the Spirit in his own life—the Spirit produces the fruits of love, joy, peace, patience, kindness, goodness, faithfulness, gentleness and self-control, which were now being tested in prison as he faced his own execution. *'Being filled with'* puts us in mind of trees whose every branch produces in this earthly life 'the fruit' Paul described in Galatians 5:22–23" (Dunnam, *Galatians, Ephesians, Philippians, Colossians, Jude,* 261–66).

Question 10. Application questions like this one are not meant to get negative, self-condemning responses. Help set the tone by sharing how your joy centers on the gospel of Christ, and prepare the way for others to do the same. Such responses will be encouraging and edifying. Also, make room and safety for honest reflection, self-evaluation, and expression of need for change.

Study 5

JOY IN GOD'S DISCIPLINE

Hebrews 12:1–13

Purpose: To understand the purpose of God's discipline in our lives and to learn to rejoice in this discipline.

Question 2. "Though Christians have such a great multitude of glorious examples of enduring faith to encourage them, they must be ever watchful of obstructions which, unless removed, will certainly impede their progress. Those hindrances are first likened to 'weights' which must be laid aside. The Greek word *ogkon,* weight, in the athletic world of that day was connected with bulk of body or superfluous flesh which had to be removed by right training. But the use of the aorist, *apothemenoi,* lay aside, suggests something which can be thrown off like a garment, which in any race would be a great hindrance. *Ogkon* is used in a general sense suggesting that the Christian must throw off every hindrance in the race" (R. V. W. Tasker, *The Epistle to the Hebrews,* Tyndale New Testament Commentaries [Grand Rapids, Mich.: Eerdmans, 1979], 189).

Other principles for running: (1) set your eyes on the goal, (2) be encouraged by Jesus' example, (3) be willing to persevere.

Anyone who has attended a cross-country race has seen these principles of running in action. They have seen the cloud of witnesses make a positive difference as they cheer their runners on. Runners carry nothing extra, wear lightweight shoes and shorts in order to make the best possible progress in the race, and keep their eyes focused on the finish line, looking neither to the left nor to the right nor behind.

Question 3. This question refers to *us* rather than *you* in order to make the discussion a bit "safer." If someone chooses to mention personal issues, however, feel free to allow the discussion to move in that direction.

Question 4. "As the athlete concentrates all his energies on winning the victor's prize, so the participant in the Christian race is urged . . . to do this *looking to Jesus,* that is, to be so totally involved that, with singleness of purpose and undistracted by all that is going on around him, his gaze is firmly fixed on him who is both the goal and the prize. . . .

"In looking to Jesus, then, we are looking to him who is the supreme exponent of faith, the one who, beyond all others, not only set out on the course of faith but also pursued it without wavering to the end. He, accordingly, is uniquely qualified to be the supplier and sustainer of the faith of his followers" (Philip Edgcumbe Hughes, *A Commentary on the Epistle to the Hebrews* [Grand Rapids, Mich.: Eerdmans, 1977], 521–23).

Question 6. Look closely at verses 5–11. We should be encouraged because it means that we are his children, that he is treating us like sons and daughters. God's discipline is a demonstration of his love. It is encouraging because God is the God of our spirits and is working on getting our spirits in shape. The results of God's discipline are also encouraging (see vv. 10–11). He disciplines us for our good.

Question 7. The phrase *share in his holiness* needs to be looked at and discussed carefully. What does the word *holy* mean?

"The Old Testament applies the word 'holy' to human beings in virtue of their consecration to religious purposes, e.g. priests who were consecrated by special ceremonies, and even to the whole nation of Israel as a people separated from the nations and consecrated to God. . . .

"But as the conception of holiness advanced . . . it took on a strong ethical significance, and this is its main, and practically its exclusive, connotation in the New Testament. . . . 'Be ye holy' is the divine call to His creatures to become partakers of His holiness (Hebrews 12:10). It is this imparting of the divine holiness which takes place in the soul of man in regeneration and becomes the spring and foundation of holy character.

"Christ in His life and character is the supreme example of the divine holiness. In Him it consisted in more than mere sinlessness: it was His entire consecration to the will and purpose of God, and to this end Jesus sanctified Himself (John 17:19). The holiness of Christ is both the standard of the Christian character and its guarantee" (*The New Bible Dictionary*, 530).

Question 9. Words like *feeble, weak, lame, disabled, healed* all indicate the need for physical therapy. Spiritually speaking, we are lame. God's discipline is like physical therapy designed to strengthen our feeble arms and weak knees. By cooperating with God's therapy, we can be healed. But if we resist because the discipline is too painful or difficult, we can become permanently disabled. Many patients going through physical therapy to recover from some physical injury simply do not do their exercises—and therefore do not improve, at least in a timely fashion. Perseverance is needed through the discipline for its work to be accomplished.

Study 6

JOY IN CHRIST'S REST

Matthew 11:28–30

Purpose: To consider and respond to Jesus' invitation to rest.

Question 1. Usually, approach questions are not meant to move as deeply as this one into a person's life and feelings. However, the group has been together for five previous studies and will probably be ready for a greater openness. The introduction to this study should also prepare them for this question.

Hopefully, deep longings and yearnings will flow at the beginning of this study. Allowing group members to become aware of their need is a big step toward their embracing the rest that Jesus offers.

However, only you will know where your group is at this point and whether this approach question is appropriate. You can help set an environment of openness and safety by sharing your longings and yearnings. If necessary, you might use a substitute question like, "In what ways would you like to experience greater rest in your life?"

Question 2. "Incomparable, ravishing sounds these—if ever such were heard in this weary, groaning world! What gentleness, what sweetness is there in the very style of the invitation—'Come unto me'; and in the words, 'All ye that toil and are burdened . . . Take my yoke upon you'—the yoke of subjection to Jesus—'and learn of me; for I am meek and lowly in heart: and ye shall find rest unto your souls'—As Christ's willingness to empty Himself to the uttermost . . . was the spring of ineffable rest to His own Spirit, so in the same track does He invite all to follow Him, with the assurance of the same experience" (Jamieson, Fausset, and Brown, *Commentary on the Whole Bible* [Grand Rapids, Mich.: Zondervan, 1976], 921).

Question 4. This question is appropriate for both Christians and non-Christians. If you have nonbelievers in the group, allow them to share why it is difficult to come. Sometimes the issue is the absence of humility—being able to admit need. Some find it difficult to believe that Jesus is who he says he is or that he will do what he says he will do. One evening two men who were not Christians were sitting around our table. One of them began asking the other why he had not yet become a Christian!

Even if we have come to Jesus for salvation, there are many reasons why we do not come to him in our Christian lives. Try to create a climate of honesty and openness as you look closely at this issue.

Question 5. A. W. Tozer gives insight in his classic book *The Pursuit of God* into the weariness and burdens that Jesus might have had in mind. He writes,

"Let us examine our burden. It is altogether an interior one. It attacks the heart and the mind and reaches the body only from within. First, there is the burden of *pride.* The labor of self-love is a heavy one indeed. Think for yourself whether much of your sorrow has not arisen from someone speaking slightingly of you.

". . . *the burden of pretense.* By this I mean not hypocrisy, but the common human desire to put the best foot forward and hide for the world our real inward poverty. . . . There is hardly a man or woman who dares to be just what he or she is without doctoring up the impression. The fear of being found out gnaws like rodents within their hearts.

". . . Another source of burden is *artificiality.* I am sure that most people live in secret fear that some day they will be careless and by chance an enemy or friend will be allowed to peep into their poor empty soul. So they are never relaxed" ([Harrisburg, Pa.: Christian Publications, 1982], 111–14).

Question 7. "*Yoke:* 1. a wooden frame or bar with loops or bows at either end, used for harnessing together a pair of oxen, etc. 2. a pair of oxen harnessed together: as, a yoke of oxen. 3. any mark or symbol of bondage or servitude. 4. subjection; bondage; servitude" (*Webster's New World Dictionary of the American Language*).

Question 8. What does Jesus promise to those who respond to his invitation? "Such a burden as this is not necessary to bear. Jesus calls us to His rest, and meekness is His method. The meek man cares not at all who is greater than he, for he has long ago decided that the esteem of the world is not worth the effort.

"The heart of the world is breaking under this load of pride and pretense. There is not release from our burden apart from the meekness of Christ" (Tozer, *The Pursuit of God,* 112, 116).

Question 9. "Rest in verses 28 and 29 . . . would perhaps be more accurately, and less misleadingly, translated 'relief'. Certainly Jesus does not promise His disciples a life of inactivity or repose, nor freedom from sorrow and struggle, but He does assure them that, if they keep close to Him, they will find relief from such crushing burdens as crippling anxiety, the sense of frustration and futility, and the misery of a sin-laden conscience" (R. T. France, *The Gospel according to St. Matthew,* Tyndale New Testament Commentaries [Grand Rapids, Mich.: Eerdmans, 1985], 122).

Tozer had some additional views on what it means to find rest. For those filled with pride and self-love, "he develops toward himself a kindly sense of humor and learns to say, 'Oh, so you have been overlooked?

"Then he will also get the deliverance from the burden of *pretense*. . . .

"To all the victims of the gnawing disease Jesus says, 'Ye must become as little children.' For little children do not compare; they receive direct enjoyment from what they have without relating it to something else or someone else.

"*Artificiality* is one curse that will drop away the moment we kneel at Jesus' feet and surrender ourselves to His meekness. Then we will not care what people think of us so long as God is pleased. Then *what we are* will be everything; what we appear will take its place far down the scale of interest for us. Apart from sin we have nothing of which to be ashamed. Only an evil desire to shine makes us want to appear other than we are" (Tozer, *The Pursuit of God,* 112–16).

Question 10. "The gracious invitation which brings chapter XI to a close is recorded only by Matthew. It is addressed in the first instance to those upon whose backs the Pharisees were laying heavy burdens by demanding meticulous obedience not only to the law itself but to their own intricate elaborations of it. Every law-abiding person is of necessity under a yoke, and the expression 'the yoke of the law' was a commonplace in Judaism (cf. Acts XV. 10). Jesus the Messiah also calls His disciples to accept a 'yoke', but how different is His yoke! In the first place it is not really obedience to any external law at all, for it is first and foremost loyalty to a Person, which enables the disciple to do gladly, and therefore easily, and without feeling that he is struggling under a heavy burden, what that Person would have him to do. If men loved Him, Jesus said, they would inevitably keep His commandments (see Jn XIV. 15, RSV). Where a relationship exists between a disciple and Himself (His) *yoke is easy and* (His) *burden is light.* Moreover, the way of life that He desires His disciples to follow is His own life. In consequence, the Christian's guide to conduct is no law-book full of baffling perplexities but the *exemplum Christi.* Learn of me is His instruction" (France, *Matthew,* 121–122).

Question 11. "And to be a pupil of Jesus is to have a very gentle and humble-minded Teacher, who is never impatient with those who are slow to learn and never intolerant with those who stumble. It would of course be boastful for any merely human teacher to claim gentleness and humility as his primary qualifications. But Jesus the Christ does not hesitate to do so. 'Learn from me,' He says, 'for I am gentle and lowly in heart' (RSV). It is precisely this feature of the divine invitation which renders it, in the description of it in the Book of Common Prayer, a 'comfortable word'; for we all know from experience that it has been the teachers who have possessed something of these lovely qualities who have most influenced us for the better. It is surely very significant that these are the characteristics of Jesus that Paul singles out as the qualities he himself would most desire to show in his dealings with his converts" (France, *Matthew,* 122).

continue the transformation . . .

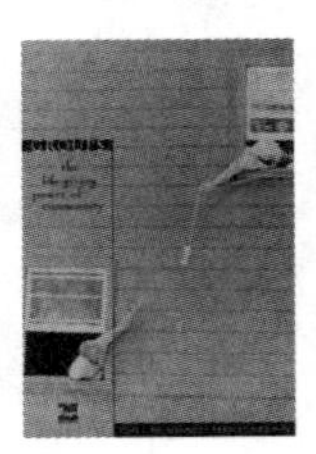

PURSUING SPIRITUAL TRANSFORMATION

JOHN ORTBERG, LAURIE PEDERSON, JUDSON POLING

Experience a radical change in how you think and how you live. Forget about trying hard to be a better person. Welcome instead to the richly rewarding process of discovering and growing into the person God made you to be! Developed by Willow Creek Community Church as its core curriculum, this planned, progressive small group approach to spiritual maturity will help you:

- Become more like Jesus
- Recapture the image of God in your life
- Cultivate intimacy with God
- Live your faith everywhere, all the time
- Renew your zest for life

Leader's guide included!

Fully Devoted: *Living Each Day in Jesus' Name*	0-310-22073-4
Grace: *An Invitation to a Way of Life*	0-310-22074-2
Growth: *Training vs. Trying*	0-310-22075-0
Groups: *The Life-Giving Power of Community*	0-310-22076-9
Gifts: *The Joy of Serving God*	0-310-22077-7
Giving: *Unlocking the Heart of Good Stewardship*	0-310-22078-5

Look for Pursuing Spiritual Transformation at your local bookstore.

www.willowcreek.com

Leading Life-Changing Small Groups

Bill Donahue / Willow Creek Resources
Foreword by Carl F. George

Like nothing else, small groups have the power to change lives. They're the ideal route to discipleship, a place where the rubber of biblical truth meets the road of human relations.

As vice president of small group ministries for the Willow Creek Association, Bill Donahue knows that small groups are key to building biblical community and thriving individuals. In *Leading Life-Changing Small Groups,* Donahue and his team share in-depth the practical insights that have made Willow Creek's small group ministry so incredibly effective.

The unique, ready-reference format of *Leading Life-Changing Small Groups* gives small group leaders, pastors, church leaders, educators, and counselors a commanding grasp of:

- Group formation and values
- Meeting preparation and participation
- Leadership requirements and responsibilities
- Discipleship within the group
- The philosophy and structure of small groups
- Leadership training

. . . and much more

From an individual group to an entire small group ministry, *Leading Life-Changing Small Groups* gives you the comprehensive guidance you need to cultivate life-changing small groups . . . and growing, fruitful believers.

Softcover 0-310-20595-6

The Fruit of the Spirit

Becoming the Person God Wants You to Be

Thomas E. Trask and Wayde I. Goodall
Foreword by Bill Bright, Founder and President of
Campus Crusade for Christ International

Would you like true fulfillment in your life? Health in your relationships? Victory over anxiety and conflict? You can have them—if you let God's Spirit grow his fruit in your heart.

In *The Fruit of the Spirit,* Tom Trask and Wayde Goodall take you for a close look at love, joy, peace, patience, kindness, and the rest of the fruit of the Spirit. Here is a passionate and illuminating look at what happens to your thoughts, emotions, and actions when you live each day in intimate relationship with Jesus Christ. Drawing from the storehouse of God's Word, Trask and Goodall sow seeds of insight into your heart that both convict and encourage.

Your witness for Christ is as good as the fruit your relationship with him produces. *The Fruit of the Spirit* points you toward a lifestyle that makes the Gospel you proclaim attractive to others because they can see its results.

Softcover 0-310-22787-9

We want to hear from you. Please send your comments about this book to us in care of the address below. Thank you.

GRAND RAPIDS, MICHIGAN 49530

www.zondervan.com